Quick-and-Easy Learning Games

Math

by Marcia K. Miller

SCHOLASTIC
PROFESSIONAL BOOKS

New York • Toronto • London • Auckland • Sydney

Dedication

Love to Mom and Dad in their 50th anniversary year

Acknowledgments

I'd like to express my thanks to all the students I've worked with over the years,
who remind me that playing is one of the best ways to learn.
And a special wink to the ones who ask, "Aren't we doing math today?"

Editor: Joan Novelli
Cover design by Jaime Lucero and Vincent Ceci
Cover and interior illustration by Paige Billin-Frye
Interior design by Sydney Wright

ISBN 0-590-96374-0

A favorite time in my math classes has always been Games Day, when children choose from the many games available to them and then play. Play? In math class? Why, of course! Given an array of purposeful games, both commercial and teacher-made, children can enjoy themselves while exploring math ideas in an informal context. To them, Games Day doesn't feel like real math—but not to worry. Playing math games addresses many under-utilized aspects of mathematics and emphasizes different learning modes. Adding games to your classroom can broaden any curriculum.

My goal in writing this book is to present teachers with ideas for games children can play to stimulate their thinking, enhance problem-solving skills, develop communication and interpersonal skills, explore other dimensions of mathematics, and have a good time in the process. Ready, set, have fun!

Best regards,
Marcia K. Miller

Contents

About this Book

When children play games, they experience entertainment, relaxation, excitement, companionship, competition, cooperation, and fun. Good recreational games rarely cause players to feel anxious or worry about looking incompetent. The same reasoning applies to good classroom games. Math games can challenge the mind, widen the imagination, and spark the spirit while helping children follow directions, strategize, engage in math talk, and simply have fun—while barely noticing that they are learning.

Competition vs. Cooperation

By definition, a game is a contest with prescribed rules; the object in playing a game is to win according to those rules. Some of the games in this book end with someone winning. However, this competition is wholesome and is in no way meant to create an atmosphere of winning and losing. The competition you'll find stimulates and excites players through discussion, analysis of rules and strategies, and some degree of mental rigor. Many games invite cooperative play, too. For instance, a game for two opponents can be played just as well, if not better, by two-player teams, who can collaborate to discuss moves, plan strategies, and optimize their success. Children who coach each other as they play become better communicators and develop respect for divergent thinking and for teamwork. You can adapt games to reflect the style of play that works best with your students.

Games and the NCTM Standards

In its *Curriculum and Evaluation Standards for School Mathematics*, the National Council of Teachers of Mathematics (NCTM) urges teachers to help children become independent thinkers and problem solvers, develop mathematical insights, improve reasoning, and engage in math communication. Good math games support all these goals by providing children with opportunities to explore, discuss, strategize, reason, predict, make connections, discover relationships, draw conclusions, reflect, and interpret.

A Note About Commercial Games

Many commercial games work well within the math curriculum. Games that require strategy; planning ahead; finding patterns; making decisions; or working with money, numbers, shapes, time, and so on can be used effectively. Browse through toy stores and math materials catalogs for games that may enhance your classroom. Consider Othello, Connect Four, and Yahtzee, to name just a few.

What's Inside?

This book includes complete instructions for 17 different games. Each game comes with reproducible game boards, playing pieces, or other necessary materials (other than typical classroom supplies). You will also find a teacher page for each game that includes the following features:

- Players: a suggested number of children to play the game
- Math Links: key mathematical concepts or topics
- Object: a simple statement of the game's goal
- Materials: a list of everything players need to begin
- Setup: things to do before presenting the game
- To Play: easy, step-by-step instructions for the game
- Math Talk: questions to spark discussion after the game
- Variations: ideas for modifying the game (for example, suggestions for playing a cooperative version or making the game easier/more challenging)

A Glossary of Terms

Some terms appear repeatedly throughout the teacher pages. Use this glossary to help you interpret them as they are used in this book.

Chips: Small counters, markers, or game pieces used to cover spaces on a game board, keep track of turns or scores, and so on. You can substitute buttons, dried beans, or any objects that can be sorted by color, shape, or other characteristic.

Crayons: Markers, colored pencils, or crayons in assorted colors.

Determine order of play: Any random generator, such as a coin toss, roll of a number cube, spin of a spinner, selection of a number from a bag of number tiles, alphabetical order, or any other fair method children may know.

Form game groups: Divide children into groups, pairs, teams, or whatever suits the game. You can create the groups, children can select their teammates or opponents, or games groups can be formed at random.

Number cubes: For most games that call for number cubes, you can use commercial dice with spots or numbers, or label classroom cubes with the numbers or symbols required for any particular game. (See page 12 for cube pattern.)

Parallel play: In some games, players need not take turns, but may move at their own pace toward a goal. (See Decide the Digits, page 13.)

Players: This term varies by game. Players may be individuals in a one-on-one situation, or pairs or small teams who can talk to one another as they play, discussing strategies and sharing ideas to optimize the outcome.

Tips for Classroom Use

- Make multiple copies of games if you want more than one group of children to be able to play at the same time. Tape game boards that appear on two pages together. Laminate game boards or paste to tag board.

- Prepare resealable bags with all necessary materials for each game. Label the bags and keep them available for use during free time, as well as during math classes. You might send game bags home overnight so children can play with family members.

- Set aside times in your daily or weekly schedule for math games, or add the choice of math games to the menu of activities from which children routinely choose.

- Adjust the rules, vary the materials, simplify the language, or change the number of players to fit your needs.

- Play demonstration games with children to model how to play. Discuss the rules as necessary until children feel ready to play on their own.

- Invite students to teach peers how to play. Teaching is a great way to learn!

- Take time to play with children yourself. Although you may be a better player, level the field by giving hints, allowing children to rethink a risky move or warning them of an upcoming situation they may not foresee. Thoughtful questions and judicious hints help children become more confident players and can help with assessment, giving you clues to the strategies children use, and so on.

- Use math games as the basis for stories, poems, journal entries, discussions, or other extensions that may arise naturally from them.

- Plan a Games Night for an open house night. Invite adults to play the games the children play to better appreciate the value of math games.

Resources

This list suggests books you may find helpful. Each provides games, activities, investigations, and other hands-on ideas for classroom use.

Board Games Round the World by Robbie Bell and Michael Cornelius (Cambridge University Press, 1988)

Family Math by Jean Kerr Stenmark, et al (Regents, University of California, 1986)

Games for Math by Peggy Kaye (Random House, 1993)

The Good Time Math Event Book by Marilyn Burns (Creative Publications, 1977)

Making Numbers Make Sense by Ron Ritchart (Addison-Wesley, 1994)

Mathematics Games for Fun and Practice by Alan Barson (Addison-Wesley, 1992)

Math for Girls and Other Problem Solvers by Diane Downie, et al (Regents, University of California, 1981)

The Mathworks by Carol Greenes, et al (Creative Publications, 1979)

Mega-Fun Math Games by Dr. Michael Schiro (Scholastic Professional Books, 1995)

The Multicultural Game Book by Louise Orlando (Scholastic Professional Books, 1993)

More or Less

Players: 2 or 4

Math Links: number sense, spatial/visual/logical reasoning, math symbols (<, =, >, ≠)
Object: to cover any three numbers in a row on the game board

MATERIALS

game board (see page 10)
symbol cube (see page 11)
number cube (see page 12)
chips in two colors

SETUP

▲ Review the meaning of the math symbols <, =, >, and ≠.

▲ Prepare the game board and symbol cube. Write the numbers 1 to 6 on the faces of the blank cube (page 12). Or, if you have one-inch cubes, you can cut self-stick labels or masking tape to label the faces of one to make a symbol cube and another with the numbers 1 to 6 to make a number cube.

TO PLAY

1 Give each player chips of one color for covering numbers on the game board.

2 In turn, players roll the symbol cube and number cube to make a math statement, such as ≠ 5. The player uses a chip to cover any open number on the board that fits the statement. (In this example, the player may cover any open number less than 5 or greater than 5, but not 5 itself.) Once placed, a chip cannot be moved.

3 Players may cover only one number per turn. If no open number fits the statement, the player loses that turn.

4 The first player to place three chips in a row horizontally, vertically, or diagonally wins.

Math Talk
• Why are there numbers such as 8 and 11 on the game board?
• What helps you decide which number to cover?
• Describe any good strategies you have found for playing.

Variations
• Make new game boards and cubes with different numbers.
• Let players roll two cubes and choose which number to use in the math statement.
• Change the object: Cover four numbers in a row.

More or Less
Game Board

More or Less

Symbol Cube

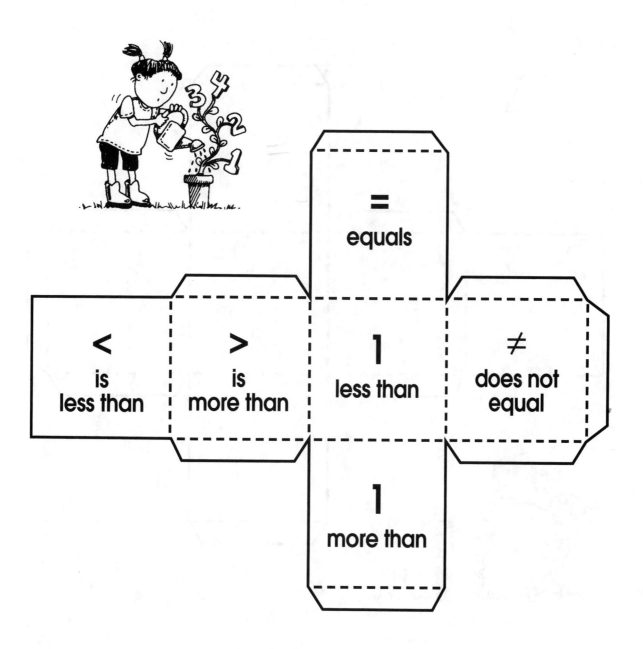

		= equals	
< is less than	> is more than	1 less than	≠ does not equal
		1 more than	

More or Less
Number Cube

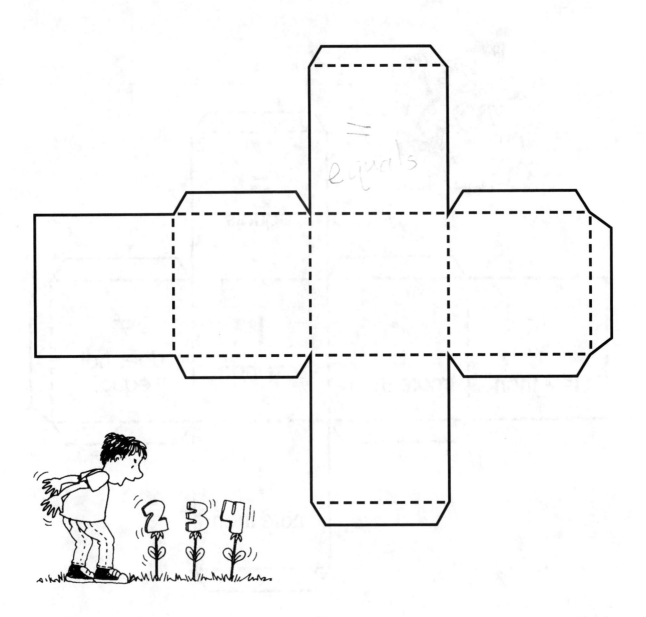

Decide the Digits

Math Links: numeration, number sense, logical reasoning
Object: to build the greatest possible number

MATERIALS

number cards (see page 14)
place value board (see page 15)

SETUP

▲ Duplicate one set of number cards for each player onto heavy paper, construction paper, or oaktag for durability and opacity. Cut them apart to make a digit deck for each player.

▲ Prepare a place value board for each player.

TO PLAY

1 Give each player a digit deck and a place value board. Have players shuffle the cards and place their decks facedown on the table.

2 This game allows for parallel play. Players draw a card from their deck and place it in any open column on their place value board. For example, a 4 can be placed to represent 4 ones, 4 tens, 4 hundreds, or 4 thousands. Once placed, a digit card cannot be moved.

3 Play continues until a four-digit number is formed. The player who has formed the greatest number earns a point for that round.

4 Digit cards are removed from the place value board, the deck is reshuffled, and play continues in the same way. The first player to earn 7 points (or any other number of points you determine) wins.

Math Talk
• What helps you decide where to place digits?
• Where would you place a zero? Why? What is the worst place for a zero?
• At what point can you tell which person will end up with the greatest number?
• What strategies help you form greater numbers?

Variations
• Let children play independently or with a partner to form their own greatest numbers.
• For younger children, use fewer places on the place value board, such as ones and tens.
• Expand the place value board to include ten thousands and hundred thousands places.
• Keep a class tally of all numbers formed to determine the greatest number anyone forms.

Decide the Digits
Number Cards

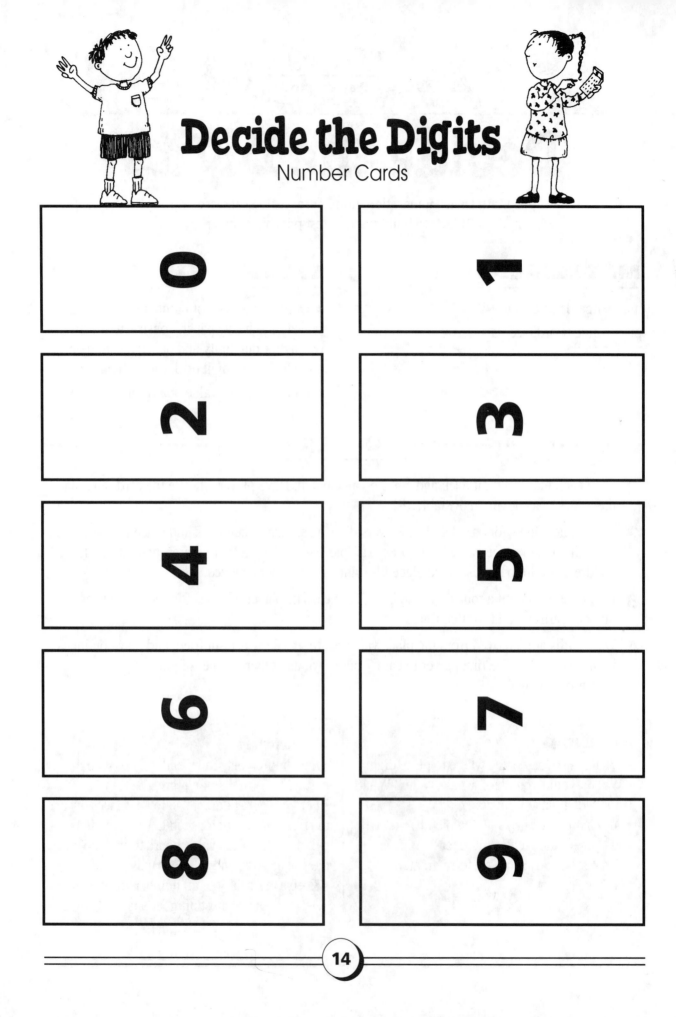

Decide the Digits

Place Value Board

thousands	hundreds	tens	ones
3000	700	50	9 = 3,759
6,000	500	10	7 6,517
9,000	300	70	8 = 9,378
1,000	400	20	6 = 1,420

Number Scrabble

Math Links: numeration, number sense, place value, number patterns and relationships, logical reasoning
Object: to use up tiles by placing them on a hundred board

MATERIALS

hundred board (see page 17)

tile bag (optional)

index cards (optional)

SETUP

▲ Review the hundred board layout.

▲ Prepare a set of tiles for each group by duplicating a hundred board onto sturdy paper. (Numbers must not be visible through the paper when tiles are facedown.) Laminate if desired. Cut apart the numbers to make a set of tiles.

▲ Duplicate a hundred board for each group.

TO PLAY

1 Form game groups. Give each group a set of number tiles and a hundred board. Players put all tiles facedown on the table or in a bag. Each player draws seven tiles at random for his or her rack. To hide their tiles from view, players can fold index cards in half the long way to form a visual barrier.

2 To begin, each player in turn places a tile on its matching number anywhere on the hundred board. This is the first phase of the game.

3 In future turns, players place a remaining tile so that it touches any tile already on the board. The new tile may touch horizontally, vertically, or diagonally. A player who can't place a tile draws a new tile from the kitty and his or her turn ends. The first to use up his or her tiles wins.

Math Talk
• How many possible places are there to put down a tile so that it touches a number not on the edges of the board?
• What helps you decide where to place your first number tile?
• Describe any good strategies you have found for playing.

Variations
• Add two blank tiles to the set; as in regular Scrabble, players may use blanks as wild cards.
• Encourage children to add new rules, such as allowing a bonus turn for placing any corner number, or allowing players to place a newly picked tile, if they can.
• Use only part of the board, such as 1 to 50; adjust the number tiles accordingly.

Number Scrabble

Hundred Board

1	2	3	4	5	6	7	8	9	10
11	12	13	14	15	16	17	18	19	20
21	22	23	24	25	26	27	28	29	30
31	32	33	34	35	36	37	38	39	40
41	42	43	44	45	46	47	48	49	50
51	52	53	54	55	56	57	58	59	60
61	62	63	64	65	66	67	68	69	70
71	72	73	74	75	76	77	78	79	80
81	82	83	84	85	86	87	88	89	90
91	92	93	94	95	96	97	98	99	100

LU-LU:
A Polynesian adding game

Math Links: addition, comparing numbers, probability (intuitive)
Object: to accumulate a target sum

MATERIALS

four Lu-Lu stones per group
permanent markers
paper and pencil

SETUP

▲ Prepare Lu-Lu stones. You may use buttons, pieces of hardened clay, flat stones, or other objects that will fall on one side or the other. Leave the front of each blank; use permanent markers to mark the backs as shown to the left.

TO PLAY

1 Form game groups. Give each group a set of Lu-Lu stones and paper and pencil.

2 Players agree on a target total, such as 50 or 100. Players take turns. The first player shakes the four Lu-Lu stones in his or her hands, spills them out, and finds the total of dots that show. The player records the sum on a score sheet.

3 Any stone that falls blank side up is shaken and spilled by the next player as a bonus. That player may add any of these bonus points to the score in his or her upcoming turn. For instance, if Kim spills a 3, a 4, and two blanks, her score is 7. Juan may shake and spill the two blank stones, record any resulting sum, then take his regular turn with all four stones, and combine both sums to get his score for that round. Any blanks spilled as a bonus do not entitle the next player to spill extra stones. For example, if Juan spills one blank as his bonus, and then two blanks in his regular spill, the next player gets to spill two stones as a bonus, not three.

4 A player who gets 10 points in a turn wins a free spill with all four stones. The first player to reach or exceed the target score wins.

Math Talk
• Why are scores different for each turn?
• What is the highest score someone can get in a single turn? (Don't forget about blanks from the player before.)
• How do you find your sum quickly?

Variations
• Make it easier: Mark three stones with 1 to 3 dots. Eliminate bonus spills. Try a harder game: Mark five stones 1 to 5. Keep the bonus spills.
• Play a cooperative version, with children combining scores on a single score sheet.

Some Sums

Math Links: addition, number sense, mental math, logical reasoning
Object: to cover all numbers on the game board

MATERIALS

game board (see page 20)

two number cubes (see page 12)

chips

SETUP

▲ Prepare the game board and number cubes. (Write the numbers 1 to 6 on each of the cubes.)

······ TO PLAY ······

1 Form game groups. Give each player a game board and some chips. Groups can share number cubes.

2 In turn, each player rolls the number cubes and finds their sum. Using chips, the player covers either one number on the game board for the sum rolled or any two numbers that give that sum. For example, a player who rolls 4 and 2 may cover 6 or 4 and 2 or 5 and 1. (Although 3 and 3 make 6, there is only one 3 on the game board.) Once a number is covered, the chip cannot be moved.

3 Players drop out when they cannot cover numbers for a given roll. At that point, they find the sum of all uncovered numbers on their game board. This sum becomes their score for the round.

4 When all players have dropped out, they compare scores, with the lowest score winning.

Math Talk

• What is the lowest possible score a player can get for a round? Explain.
• How can it be that the last person able to play is not the winner?
• Which are the hardest numbers on the game board to cover? Why?
• Describe any good strategies you have found for playing.

Variations

• Have groups play on one board, working cooperatively to cover all numbers.
• Make different number cubes with numbers such as 0 to 5 or 3 to 8. Use the new number cubes with the same game board, or create alternate game boards.
• Allow children to cover one, two, or three numbers that give a sum.

Some Sums
Game Board

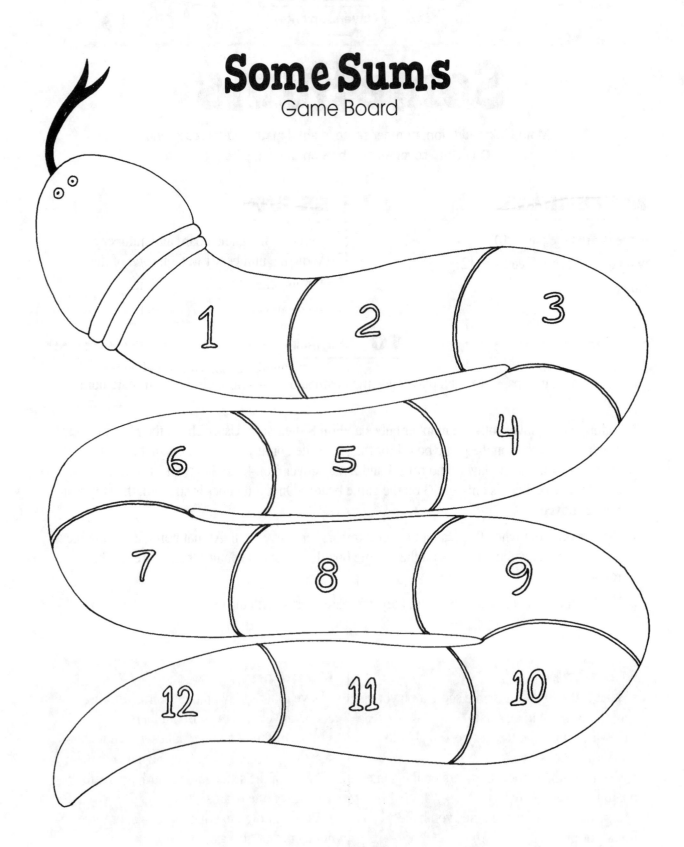

Target Math

Math Links: addition
Object: to accumulate the greatest score

MATERIALS

game board (see page 22)

chips

paper and pencil

SETUP

▲ Prepare the game board by duplicating it on oaktag or construction paper and laminating for durability and ease of sliding.

▲ Discuss the layout of the game board. In turn, children will be sliding or flicking a chip from the start space to see where it lands. Talk with children about safe and effective ways to take their turns.

TO PLAY

1 Form game groups. Give each group a game board, chips, and paper and pencil.

2 In turn, each player slides or flicks a chip from the START space so that it lands on the target. The score is the sum of all numbers the chip touches. If the chip misses the target, the player may have another try. If the chip misses on the second try, the player's turn ends.

3 Play continues until everyone has played five rounds. At that point, the player with the greatest score wins.

Math Talk

• What are the most numbers you'd ever have to add to find your score for one turn?

• Toward which part of the board do you aim your chip? Why?

• Describe any good strategies you have found for playing.

Variations

• Have children play cooperatively to earn a high score together.

• Have children predict how many turns it will take to reach a target score.

• Have children design similar but original game boards.

• Invite children to create new rules, such as getting bonus points for landing completely within a space, or losing points for missing the board.

Target Math

Game Board

		10				
	9	8	9			
	8	7	8			
	7	6	5	6	7	
	6	5	4	5	6	
5	4	3	2	3	4	5
4	3	2	1	2	3	4

START

Make a Difference

Math Links: subtraction, numeration, number sense, logical reasoning
Object: to select a pair of numbers that give the greatest difference

MATERIALS

game board (see page 24)

number cubes (see page 12)

paper and pencil

manipulatives (i.e., place value blocks)

calculator (optional)

SETUP

▲ Review the meanings of *row* and *difference*.

▲ Prepare the game board and number cubes. (Write the numbers 1 to 6 on two blank cubes.)

TO PLAY

1 Form game groups. Give each group a game board, two number cubes, paper and pencil, and manipulatives. Explain that players will take turns selecting two numbers from the game board and then subtracting to find the difference between them.

2 In turn, players roll the number cubes to represent rows from which to select numbers. For example, a roll of 3 and 6 means that the player can choose any number from Row 3 and another from Row 6 to find the difference between them. If a player rolls doubles, both numbers must be selected from that row.

3 Once rows have been determined and numbers selected, the player completes the subtraction using paper and pencil, manipulatives, mental math, or a calculator. Partners may check each other's computation.

4 The player whose numbers give the greatest difference earns a point for that round. The first player to earn 5 points wins.

Math Talk

• How do you know which number to subtract?
• What do you notice about numbers that give greater differences?
• Do larger numbers always give greater differences? Explain.

Variations

• Make new game boards. Simplify the game by using smaller numbers; increase the challenge by including three-digit numbers.
• Have children play cooperatively to get the greatest total difference after five rounds, then compare totals after several games.

Make a Difference

Game Board

7	26	58	89	49	6
52	23	8	10	77	47
2	38	25	61	0	70
66	41	1	39	80	4
5	12	74	64	86	10
17	3	20	33	9	55

Row 1
Row 2
Row 3
Row 4
Row 5
Row 6

Rectangle Race

Math Links: multiplication, addition, area, visual/spatial reasoning
Object: to fill the greatest possible area on the game grid

MATERIALS

game grid (see page 26)

number cubes (see page 12)

crayons

SETUP

▲ Review the characteristics of rectangles. Remind children that a square is a particular kind of rectangle.

▲ Duplicate a game grid for each player. Prepare the number cubes. (Write the numbers 1 to 6 on each cube.)

TO PLAY

1 Form game groups. Give each group crayons (a different color for each player) and two number cubes to share. All players need their own game grids.

2 In turn, players roll the number cubes for the dimensions of a rectangle to shade on the grid. For example, a player who rolls 3 and 5 may shade a 3 x 5 rectangle or a 5 x 3 rectangle anywhere it will fit. Rectangles may border each other or abut the edge of the grid, but may not overlap or extend past the game grid.

3 Play continues until a player doesn't have enough space to shade his or her required rectangle. At that point, everyone finds the total number of grid boxes (1 x 1 squares) shaded on their game grids. The player who has shaded the greatest number of squares (area) wins.

Math Talk

• How do you decide where to shade your rectangle?

• What shows that a 3 x 4 or a 4 x 3 rectangle cover the same amount of space?

• What other way can you determine the winner?

• Describe any good strategies you have found for playing.

Variations

• Use a smaller, larger, or nonsquare game grid; make number cubes with different numbers, such as 0 to 5 or 2 to 7.

• Have players work cooperatively to cover as much area as possible on one grid.

Rectangle Race
Game Grid

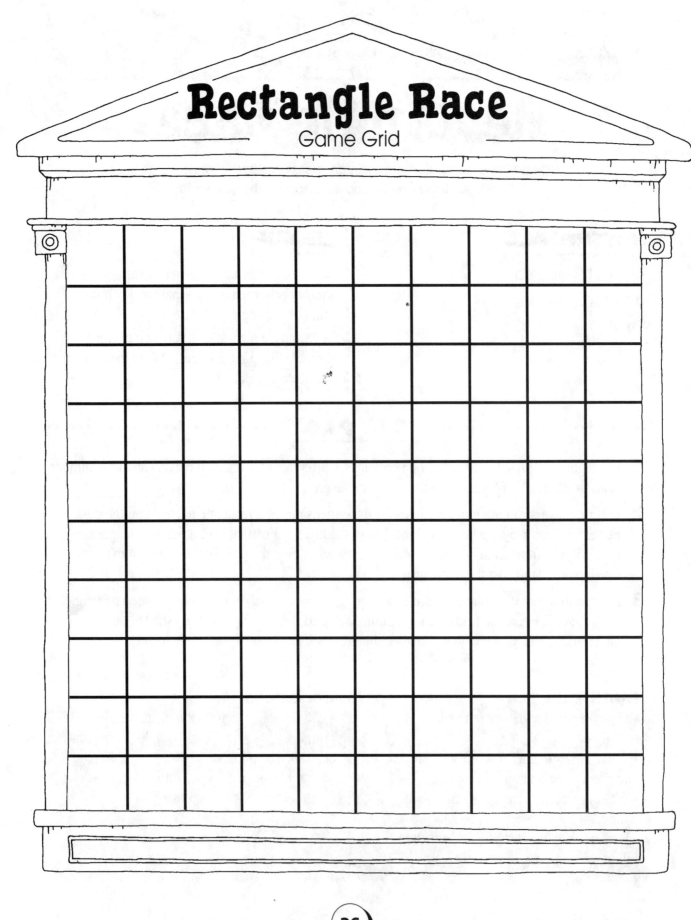

Lost Lamb

Math Links: coordinate geometry, logical/visual/spatial reasoning
Object: to find a lamb hidden on a coordinate grid

MATERIALS

game grid (see page 28)
number cubes (see page 12)
crayons
barriers (books or folders)

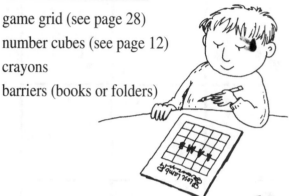

SETUP

▲ Review how to name and find ordered pairs on a coordinate grid.

▲ Prepare a game grid for each player.

▲ You may want to play a game with children to model how to hide the lamb, name points as ordered pairs, and mark grids to remember what ordered pairs have already been guessed.

TO PLAY

1 Players shield their coordinate grids from opponents' view. Each player secretly hides a lamb anywhere on the grid by writing the letters L-A-M-B on any four points in a horizontal or vertical row.

2 Players try to find their opponents' lost lamb by naming an ordered pair, such as (2,3). If the searcher names a point on the lamb, the hider says, "*Baaaaa.*" A correct guess allows the searcher another guess. If the ordered pair is not on the lamb, the hider says, "No" and that searcher's turn ends. Players switch roles and continue in turn.

3 The first player to locate all four letters of the lost lamb wins.

Math Talk

• Why is it important in this game to say numbers in a certain order?
• How do you keep track of your guesses?
• What strategy do you use for new guesses?
• What patterns can you notice in the ordered pairs that locate the lamb?
• Describe your strategies for playing.

Variations

• Allow players to hide the lamb on a diagonal, such as (1,0), (2,1), (3,2), and (4,3).
• Simplify the game by using a smaller grid, such as 4 x 4, or by hiding an animal with a longer name, such as *tiger*. Increase the challenge by using a larger grid or by hiding an animal with a shorter name, such as *pig*.

Lost Lamb
Game Grid

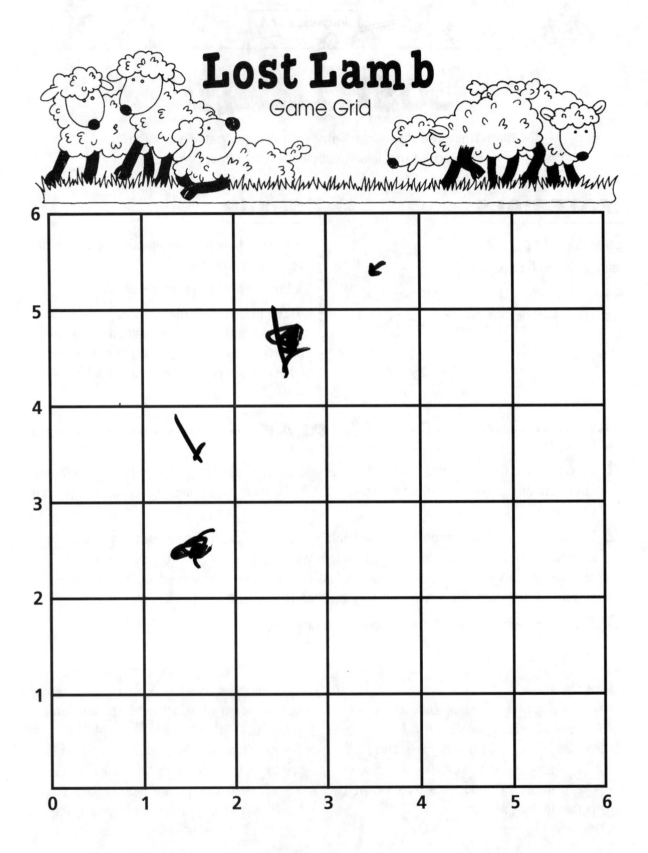

Mirror, Mirror

Players: 2 or 4

Math Links: geometry, symmetry, visual/spatial reasoning, patterns
Object: to complete the symmetrical half of a figure begun by another

MATERIALS

game board (see page 30)
pattern blocks or color tiles
(see page 31)

SETUP

▲ Review the concept of *symmetry* (equal parts of a figure that, if folded, would fit exactly on top of each other), or mirror image.

▲ Prepare pattern block cutouts. If possible, precolor the figures to look like actual pattern blocks: yellow hexagon, red trapezoid, orange square, green triangle, blue larger rhombus, tan smaller rhombus.

▲ Prepare a game board for each player.

TO PLAY

1 Provide players with pattern blocks (or color tiles) and game boards. Each player may use any ten blocks to form HALF of an original design on ONE side of the mirror (line of symmetry).

2 Players swap design halves (or change seats). Each player tries to complete the symmetrical other half of the design on the opposite side of the line of symmetry.

3 Players check one another's completed figures to see that they are symmetrical, or exact mirror images of one another.

Math Talk
• If you could, where would you fold your design to prove that both sides match exactly?
• What helps you decide which blocks to use to complete a design?
• What is tricky about this for you?
• Describe any good strategies you have found for playing.

Variations
• Rotate the game board to present children with a vertical line of symmetry.
• Use more (or fewer) than ten pattern blocks to create the half-figure.
• Draw a line of symmetry on grid paper and have children use crayons to color a half-design within the boxes.

Mirror, Mirror
Game Board

Mirror, Mirror
Pattern Blocks

Tetrominoes

Math Links: geometry, transformations (flips, turns, slides), visual/spatial/logical reasoning
Object: to place tetrominoes on the game board

MATERIALS

tetrominoes (see page 33)
game grid (see page 26)
envelopes

SETUP

▲ Prepare multiple sets of tetrominoes and a grid for each group. You may wish to have students shade each tetromino a different color.

TO PLAY

1 Form game groups. In turn, each player randomly draws a tetromino from the envelope and places it anywhere on the grid. All outer edges of the tetromino must align with grid lines.

Note: A player may turn or slide a tetromino into any orientation to fit the available space on the game grid; however, tetrominoes may not be flipped over. Tetrominoes may interlock if the configuration permits, but they may never overlap another piece or extend beyond the borders of the game grid.

2 If a player draws a tetromino that cannot fit anywhere on the grid, that player is out. Play continues until only one player remains. That player wins.

Math Talk
• What helps you decide where to place a tetromino?
• Do you think it is more fair to pick a tetromino without looking? Why?
• Which do you think is the easiest tetromino to place? The hardest? Explain.
• Describe your strategies for playing.

Variations
• Change the size of the game grid.
• Invite children to create new rules for the game, such as allowing an extra pick when a player draws a tetromino that cannot be placed, or having each player draw seven tetrominoes to start and playing until someone goes out.
• Play with pentominoes (arrangements of five adjoining squares) or triominoes (arrangements of three adjoining squares).
• Have children play cooperatively, working to cover the game grid or a portion of it.

Tetrominoes

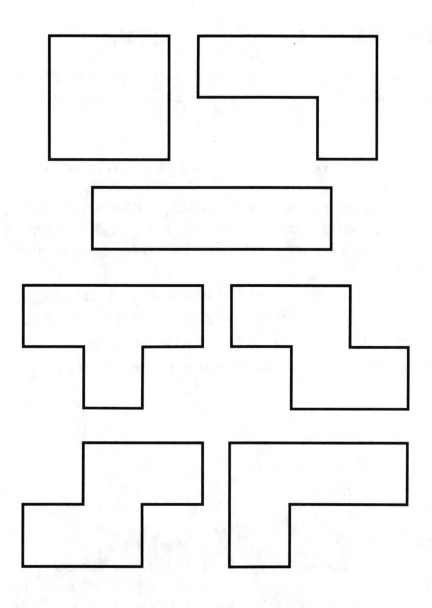

Players: any #

Toss and Tally

Math Links: addition, patterns, combinations, graphing, probability (intuitive)
Object: to chart the sum of number cube rolls to fill bars of a graph

MATERIALS

game graph (see page 35)
number cubes (see page 12)
crayons (or chips)

SETUP

▲ Duplicate a game graph for each player.
▲ Prepare number cubes. (Write in the numbers 1 to 6.)

TO PLAY

1 Any number can play this game, including individuals. Give each player a game graph, two number cubes (players can share them), and crayons. Explain that children will roll the number cubes and color in boxes to represent the sums. Have children predict which column they think will fill up first.

2 In turn, players roll the number cubes, find the sum of the roll, and color a box in the column that represents that sum. To make the game graphs reusable, players can fill boxes with chips.

3 Play continues until someone fills a column completely to the top.

4 The game may be paused in progress; play can resume at another time.

Math Talk

• Why do you think there isn't a 1 on the game graph?
• Which sums do you think are most likely to come up? Least likely? Why?
• Do you think the game graph will look the same after every game? Explain.

Variations

• Create a horizontal bar graph to vary the look of the game board.
• Have children play with three number cubes. Adjust the graph accordingly.
• Play with two-player teams.

Toss and Tally
Game Graph

| 2 | 3 | 4 | 5 | 6 | 7 | 8 | 9 | 10 | 11 | 12 |

Income, Outgo

Math Links: coin values, money notation and transactions, addition/subtraction
Object: to accumulate the most money

MATERIALS

game board (see page 37–38)

number cube (see page 12)

play coins and bills

game markers (one per player)

SETUP

▲ Review money notation. Discuss the meaning of the terms *income* (money that comes to you) and *outgo* (money that leaves you).

▲ Tape game board pages together to form one board. Write the numbers 1 to 6 on the cube.

TO PLAY

1 Form game groups, and have players select someone to serve as banker. Give each group a game board, a bank of play money, a number cube, and game markers for each player. Before the game begins, the banker gives each player $1.00 in any combination of coins or as a single bill. All game markers go on START, and players determine an order of play.

2 In turn, players roll the number cube, move that number of spaces on the board, and follow the directions on the space they land on. Players may ask the banker for change as necessary to complete a turn. Any money players win, find, earn, or borrow comes from the bank. Any money players lose, give away, spend, or lend goes to the bank.

3 If a player runs out of money before reaching FINISH, he or she may ask the bank for a one-time-only loan of 25¢. The banker keeps track of all loans. Play continues until all players reach FINISH. The player with the most money (after repaying loans) wins.

Math Talk

• Which kinds of spaces give you income? Which kinds of spaces stand for outgo?

• What helps you decide which coins to use for outgo?

• What do you think would happen if players began with no money?

Variations

• Create a similar game board with greater money amounts, different kinds of directions, more REST STOPS, and so on. Let children create their own versions of the game, too.

• Add new rules, such as: If a player lands on an occupied space, he or she must pay a 5¢ toll to the player who got there first.

Income, Outgo

Game Board

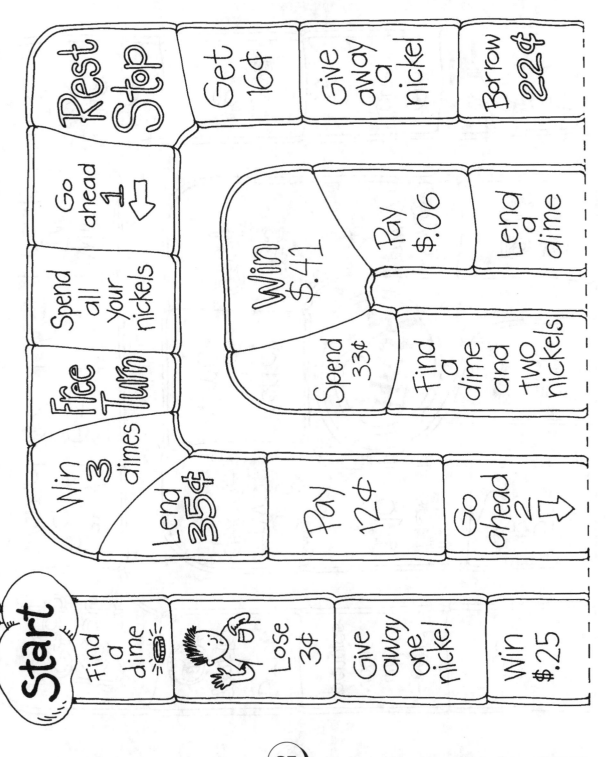

Income, Outgo

Game Board

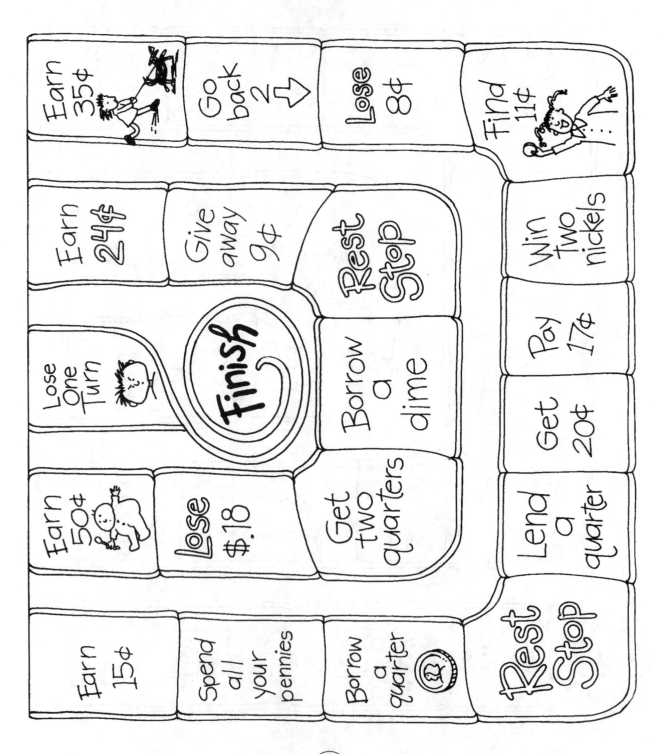

Pizza Pans

Math Links: part-whole relationships, fractions of a region, fraction estimation, equivalent fractions (intuitive), mixed numbers (intuitive), visual/spatial reasoning

Object: to use pattern blocks to fill hexagonal pizza pans

MATERIALS

pattern blocks (see page 31)

game board (see page 40)

pattern block spinner (see page 41)

SETUP

▲ Duplicate the game board and prepare the pattern block spinner by attaching the spinner with a paper fastener. The spinner works best when it is laminated or mounted on tag board.

▲ Prepare multiple sets of pattern blocks for each game group, omitting the squares and small rhombuses.

TO PLAY

1 Form game groups. Give each group a game board, a pattern block spinner, and an assortment of pattern blocks.

2 The first player spins the spinner, takes the block shown, and places it in any available space in any of the pizza pans, aligning at least one edge of the pattern block with an edge of the pan. Once placed, a pattern block may not be moved.

3 Play continues in turn. If a player spins a block that will not fit in any pan, the player may spin once more. If the next pattern block won't fit, the turn ends.

4 Play continues until someone fills the last available space in the pizza pans. That player wins.

Math Talk

• Why do you think this game is played without squares and small rhombuses?

• What is the fewest number of spins it would take to fill all the pizza pans? How likely do you think this is to happen? Explain.

• Describe any good strategies you have found for playing.

Variations

• Have children play cooperatively to fill all the pizza pans.

• Make a new game board with more (or fewer) pizza pans to fill.

• Invite children to create new rules for the game, such as: If a player places a piece that fills up a pan, he or she may take a free turn.

• Play with two-player teams.

Pizza Pans

Game Board

Pizza Pans

Pattern Block Spinner

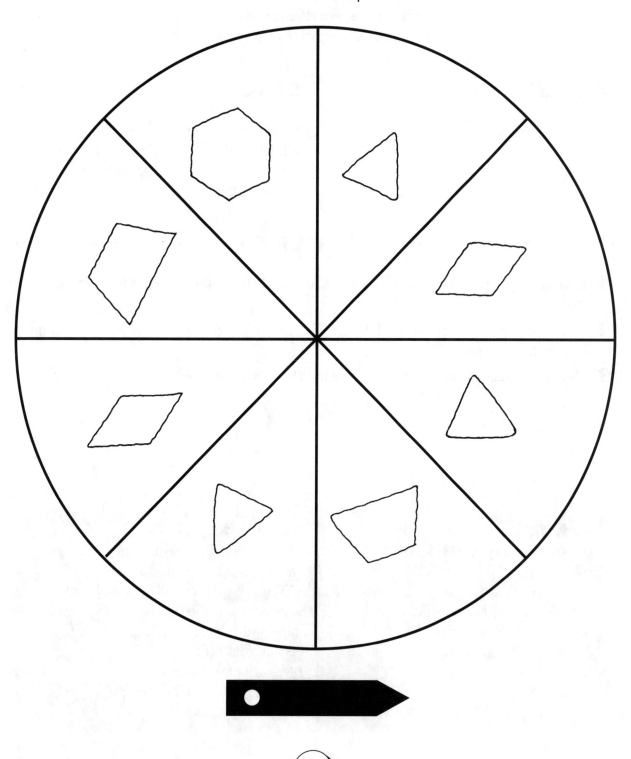

Players: 2

Last One Out

Math Links: patterns, logical/visual/spatial reasoning
Object: to strategize how not to remove the last chip

MATERIALS

game board (see page 43)
chips

SETUP

▲ Duplicate the game board.

▲ If you wish, you can talk about other games children may know that are based on the classic math game NIM.

TO PLAY

1 Form game groups. Give each group a game board and 16 chips. Ask players to cover each space with a chip.

2 In turn, players take 1 or 2 chips off the game board. If a player wants to take 2 chips, they must be from the same row.

3 Play continues until someone must take the last chip. That person loses.

Math Talk
• Do you prefer to go first or second? Explain.
• How do you think the game would change if you could take any number of chips, as long as they were in the same row?
• At what point in the game can both players tell who will win?
• Describe any good strategies you have found for playing.

Variations
• Present new rules. For example, allow players to take 1, 2, or 3 chips at a time.
• Experiment with alternate game boards—with a different total number of chips, with more (or fewer) rows, or with different numbers of chips per row.
• Play with two-player teams.
• Change the object: have the player who takes the last chip win.

Last One Out

Game Board

Line-Up
A Solomon Islands strategy game

Math Links: logical/visual/spatial reasoning, diameter and radius (intuitive)
Object: to get three chips in a straight line that passes through the center of the game board

MATERIALS

game board (see page 45)
6 chips (3 each of two colors)

SETUP

▲ Duplicate the game board.

TO PLAY

1 Form game groups. Give each group a game board and 6 chips. Ask players to cover the three squares with the chips of one color and the three triangles with the chips of the other color.

2 Players take turns moving any chip to any adjacent open space, either around the outside of the wheel or into or out of the center. In a single turn, a chip may be moved only one space from where it was.

3 The first player to position three chips of the same color in a straight line through the center of the wheel wins.

Math Talk
• Why do you need to use chips of two colors to play this game?
• What helps you decide where to move?
• Describe any good strategies you have found for playing.

Variations
• Have children play cooperatively to get three in a row in as few moves as possible.
• Make alternate game boards with 10 or 12 spaces around the wheel. Have children play with 8 or 10 chips.
• Add new rules, such as allowing a player to jump over a chip to an empty space on the other side of it.

Line-Up

Game Board

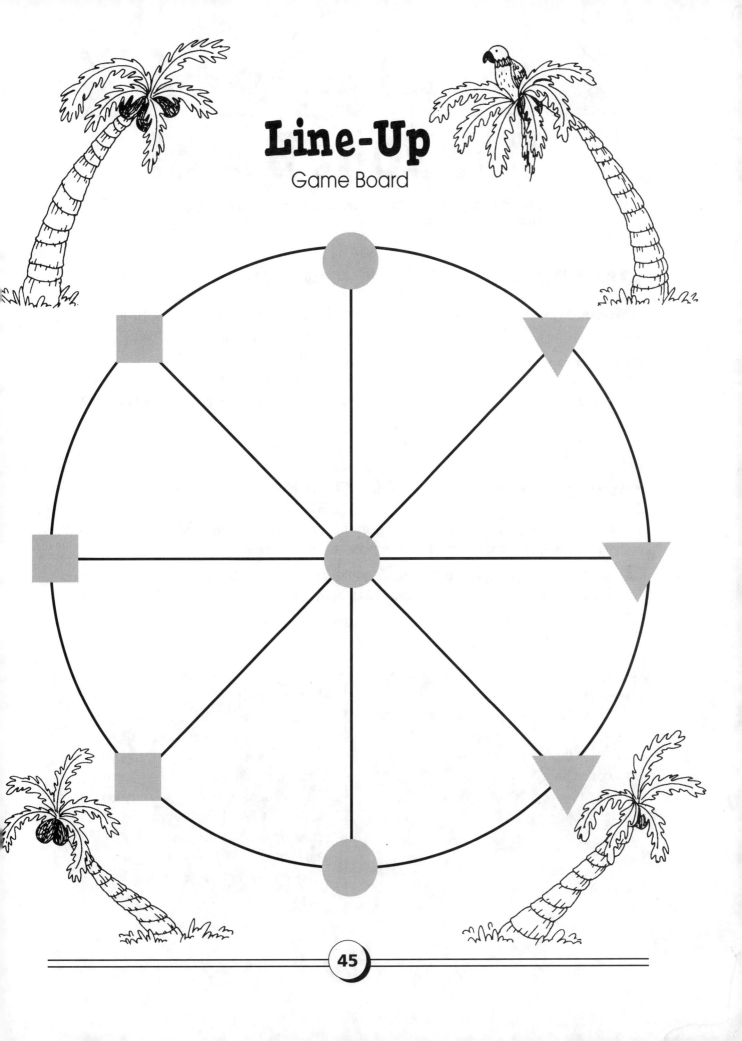

Use Your Bean!

Math Links: logical/visual/spatial reasoning, mapping theory (intuitive)
Object: to be the last person to place a bean (or chip) on the board

MATERIALS

game boards (see pages 47–48)

dried beans (or chips)

small paper cups or plates (optional)

SETUP

▲ Duplicate the game boards. Board 1 gives a basic version of the game, Board 2 presents a more challenging version.

▲ If you use dried beans, choose ones with a somewhat flat shape, such as kidney, pinto, or lima beans.

TO PLAY

1 Form game groups. Give each group a game board and a handful of dried beans (or chips) to share. You may use small paper cups or plates to hold the beans.

2 In turn, players put a bean in a fair space on the game board. A fair space is any empty space that does not touch a space that already has a bean in it.

3 Play continues until there are no more fair spaces left. The player who places the last bean wins.

Math Talk

• Why should you choose your spaces carefully?
• What is the fewest number of neighbors a space can have?
• Describe any good strategies you have found for playing.

Variations

• Reverse the rules: Tell children that each bean added to the game board (except for the first one) must touch a space that already has a bean in it.
• Have children play cooperatively to place as many (or as few) beans as possible.
• Invite children to design and play with other game boards.
• Play with two-player teams.

Use Your Bean!

Game Board 1

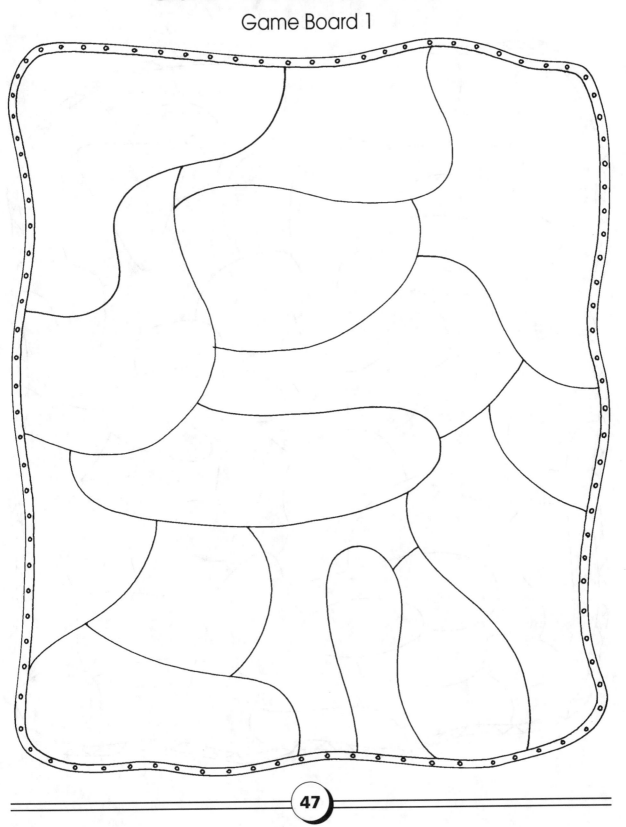

Use Your Bean!

Game Board 2